THE COMEBACK; Part One:

'Losing it all'

At 40 years old, Jayne's 17-year marriage was over, her husband blamed her business for the breakup but nothing prepared her for the painful truth.
She lost everything, and began to suffer severe mental health problems, which led to some terrifying suicidal episodes.

Fighting to overcome the loss of her business, her family life, depression, and anxiety, including a binge-eating disorder that was spiraling out of control, she overcame her obstacles and strived for a new independent life.

THE COMEBACK; Part One: 'Losing it all'

Jayne Eccles

THE COMEBACK; Part One:
'Losing it all'

Copyright © Jayne Eccles 2017
First published by Amazon Publishing 2017
This edition (2nd) 2018

ISBN 9781976766145

A CIP record is available for this book from the British Library.

I dedicate this book to my mum; she has had to act as my carer, visiting me every day. No matter how old you are, you are still your mama's baby and I turned back into a vulnerable little girl, and without her I would not be here.

Her support and unconditional love has shown me that I can't let this beat me, I have a wonderful life, I just couldn't see it through the darkness, and I was living in hell.

It has taken months to become stronger and it is a day-by-day process. One step at a time and it is important to have that support around you.

I was so excited to shower my mum with gifts to celebrate her recent 70th birthday. I booked a family holiday in the sun; she deserved to have a break after all that I have put her through. We can make some happy memories together and appreciate every single moment following such a challenging time.

She has been my biggest supporter; I love her so much and want to show her just how special she is and how grateful I am to have her in my life.

Thank you with all my heart, my precious mama x

Chapter One: My life before depression

Once upon a time there was a 21 year old girl from the North East of England, she had never believed in love at first sight until one day when she noticed a man who made her heart literally skip a beat.

He was gorgeous, the man of her dreams and she fell for him immediately, she found herself eagerly waiting for him to arrive for his daily workouts at the Health Club where she had just started working as a Customer Service Advisor.

He always arrived with his pal around 4pm and because she worked on the front desk, she watched him as he walked through the glass corridor of the reception.

She was so excited when he asked her out, absolutely smitten and there would never be another man for her, as far as she was concerned she had found her prince charming.

They quickly fell deeply in love and became inseparable. Life was great and after just a couple of years together they were married.
She felt like a real life princess on her wedding day, with a horse and carriage and walking down the aisle with her dad who gave her away to the man she adored.

But the fairytale ended after over 17 years of being his wife and a mother of his two children, the vows she had taken on that day and the belief that they would grow old together sadly was not meant to be.

The story you are about to read is my story and I am Jayne. I wanted to share my personal experience of the past year when I lost everything, including myself.

The story of my life starts in 1998 when my partner and I moved into our brand new home, it was a very happy home, we married in 2000 and I was content with looking after my man, looking after him the best I could. He always had his dinner on the table, his lunchbox made – those little things that wifey's do.

I loved being a wife and I loved my husband dearly.

We lived an ordinary married life (ordinary to us), a life similar to a million others where we both worked and shared bills.

Then in 2003 along came our beautiful daughter, she made our family complete, she was so beautiful. Of course I am biased but I remember being stopped in the street by people saying that they had never seen such a beautiful baby before, we were so blessed.

Our marriage was very loving, we respected each other and supported each other, we had our share of heartache too when I suffered a couple of consecutive miscarriages trying for baby number two. It was devastating and I remember thinking that I was living someone else's life at the time. Grief does that to you. It changes you but we got through it and thankfully, following my third pregnancy we discovered at our scan that we were having a boy, how perfect was that? A daughter and now a son on the way, we were delighted.

It wasn't until recently when I realised just how blessed I was at that time because life's struggles can dampen your perception of what you have and other things become a focus, worry, stress, debt etc.

I was always a daydreamer and growing up I believed that there was such a wonderful life waiting for me and my family one day.

I had a huge ambition but sadly this eventually became the bullet that killed my marriage, however, the person with the gun, the one who pulled the trigger is the woman my husband went off with.

Now let me put one thing straight, this book isn't revenge for such a betrayal even though I believe she planned to take my husband for a long time, this is evident as she basically confessed to pursuing him and took great pleasure in messaging me through Facebook that she had taken over my role and there was nothing I could do about it. My friends warned me about her and I knew that she secretly wanted him but never did I think he would go there but it seems that he was drawn in by her advances.

I remember the day like it was yesterday, the day she told me that she had asked him out and had been working for him for months. She was someone I classed as a friend and I even commented on one of her posts on social media the night before! However events would show her friendship was fake and I believe what she was really doing was stalking my Facebook while she got her claws into my husband.

Our marriage was going through a tough time which started when I signed up for a 2 year lease on my new fitness studio. I had big plans to make this a successful business that would make our lives amazing.

My husband became resentful of the attention I was putting into trying to establish myself as a successful business woman but ironically my hard work was all for him, he didn't see my vision and he gave me an ultimatum. I knew then that if he really loved me he would never do that. I had worked so hard, I also worked for him and supported him in his own business, helped him to grow but I wanted to follow my own dreams and earn my own money.

The plan was for me to eventually earn enough money for him to retire early because we had struggled for so long and I felt guilty that the struggle was my fault. I wanted to prove that I could make it and that one day, our lives would change for the better and we would live debt and worry free forever, going on luxury holidays and eating in fancy restaurants and the kids would want for nothing.

My business became a heavy burden and he distanced himself as the months went on, rolling his eyes at every new idea as I tried to keep my head above water and shunning my dreams like they were never going to happen. He couldn't see past it all and started turning his attention elsewhere.

It's not until I discovered his relationship with someone else that the signs where there right in front of me all along. I would never ever have looked at another man so I didn't expect his eyes to wander.

You know the classic signs as he started going out with 'a new mate' from the gym and suddenly taking extra care of his appearance.

I knew there was someone else; you don't fall out of love with your wife after 17 years just because she worked too hard. We were still intimate even though our day to day lives were stressful; we always made time for each other every weekend in fact.

Chapter Two: The beginning of the end

It was a very proud day when I signed a lease for my new fitness studio, I knew it was a risk but I was convinced that I could make it a success and the plans I had were crazy bonkers. I wanted to live an extraordinary life and never doubted myself; I worked hard without losing my passion and vision. I knew it wasn't going to happen overnight but I wasn't afraid of working above and beyond for the prospect of living a life of freedom.

I had tunnel vision and was determined to carry on regardless of the obstacles but I never imagined it would be such a strain.

Luckily, around 3 years ago when I first opened my fitness studio I planned to rent the space to other instructors so they could teach their own classes.

I received a message from someone who wanted to see if the studio was a suitable venue for her brand new business. She had huge plans but wanted a start-up space to build her Hair and Beauty Training Academy. We hit it off immediately and she became my best friend.

We both wanted the same out of life and weren't afraid to work hard to get it.

Her business was flying and rapidly grew over just a few months. My fitness studio was struggling to take off, instructors came and went and I was so desperate for it to work that I tried anything and everything, juggling too many things was a big learning curve for me but the lease was signed for 2 years and I had to try everything I could.

I really don't know what I would have done without her contribution to the rent. My stress and worry was always present but I passionately continued to do my best, this was my new business venture and I had every faith in it, however, my husband did not.

Following months of being a mother and wife while trying to establish my business, cracks began to show.

I left my husband in March 2016 because when I asked him if he loved me he said no and just walked up the stairs away from me. I was crushed but I was not going to stay in a home where I was no longer wanted; I wanted to get as far away as possible. It was obvious there was someone else in his life, he never tried to work at our marriage, he just gave up on it, it's no surprise he denied there was someone else but his behaviour proved that of a guilty man.

I was never going to find out the truth, he couldn't look me in the eye, he was uncomfortable around me and his guilt was all over his face.

The only thing I could do was to pretend that I had 'moved on' this was the only way that the truth would come out. My best mate set up a profile on a dating site initially for a confidence boost as I was in bits, I wasn't interested in a relationship but the messages came through thick and fast. I didn't have a clue about this new age dating. I had been married for so long and only had eyes for my husband.

I didn't go with anyone from the site, it was all just banter but admittedly it did distract me from the reality of my heart-wrenching split for a short while at least.

As months went on I was even more convinced that there was a secret relationship going on. I decided to make out that I was having plenty of fun with other men, which was so far from the truth. I couldn't even look at myself in the mirror let alone go dating. Moving on wasn't going to come easy to me.

He was seen (by a real friend of mine) dropping her off at a village pub. I knew who this woman was, she lived near us and she even attended classes at my fitness studio. She had her eyes on the prize for a long time and nothing was going to stop her from claiming him for herself.

She changed the man I loved into someone I no longer recognise and no longer want in my life for that matter. Secrets and lies have caused so much pain and turned my whole world upside down. I was the one accused of living a lie.

My side of the story will show the damage that their actions caused and the devastating affects it had on my family. Firstly though, let me take you through my journey over the past year following the news that my husband was the one who was actually living a lie, not me.

The truth is that your relationship started way before you slept together, an emotional affair probably went on for months where he confided in you and you were more than happy to be a shoulder to cry on. He then started to take care of his appearance and acting distant towards me, you had him right where you wanted him and it was only a matter of time before he would give in to you. When we first separated you made sure that I was deleted from his social media and I even recall me going back home and noticing that my photograph was facing the wall, I wonder whose benefit that was for?

I was forced out of my own home because you were waiting in the wings but you still had to twist the knife and tried to tarnish my reputation saying that I left my family for a failing business which was thousands of pounds in debt, you spread a lot of vicious slander that showed your true character.

I had to start my life over, in a new home, while your secret lives carried on pretty much the same. A few months into living at my new house, I started to notice my thoughts becoming unhealthy; I was struggling to cope as the realisation began to hit me. I had spent hours trawling through the Internet, looking for advice on divorce, starting over, and co-parenting. It was like a minefield.

I felt the need to reach out to my GP who had known me for many years, he helped me to see another perspective as I told him what had

happened. He also referred me to 'Talking Therapies' I found this helped me to let out my emotions and anger and after a few months, the program finished. It was just before Christmas but I felt a tad stronger.

I was dreading Christmas, we were no longer a family unit, I was in a different home other than the family home I had in lived for 18 years with so many memories.

Surprisingly, Christmas day was much better than expected surrounded by family and friends but the days following I fell deeper into depression, this time I felt enraged with anger, how could he put me through this? How could he humiliate me like this when I adored him and done my best? Now he is exchanging gifts with her.

The resentment I was feeling was very uneasy, I could have run them both over if I saw them in the street. I avoided driving past as much as possible to avoid seeing them, it hurt like hell.

New Year's Eve was very traumatic. I sent my mum home with the kids because I couldn't cope and wanted the day to end and just go to bed. I drank some wine and took some sleeping pills so that I wouldn't wake until morning; I just wanted the pain to go away.

Every day is different for me; I don't know how my feelings will change from day to day. You think you have turned a corner then the next minute you are in a heap on the floor in tears. It hits you unexpectedly; I can only describe it as torment.

No matter how hard I tried to think, OK it's a new year, time to snap out of it but that is easier said than done. Although I was determined to start again and think positive thoughts, plan ahead and stick with it, it all just turns to shit in an instant and I am back to black. Sometimes I forget that I am no longer with him but then reality kicks in and it's that feeling you get when someone close to you has passed away, it takes a moment until you get that sinking feeling of anguish.

Luckily I have started to change my thoughts in a conscious way to distract myself. It takes practice but I am reminding myself constantly, in time it will become habit and my thoughts will pass and fade but until then I just have to ride it out. It's all part of the journey, there are no short cuts and you have to feel the emotions go through you in waves, feel the pain to let it go but the letting go bit is still a curse I still cling to.

Chapter Three: My Daily Journal

JANUARY

I was at my lowest point. I was tormented by thoughts and felt trapped in my own mind, I could not let the past go, I was torturing myself and making my life hell, I was worrying my family and friends. The pain is physical; I have never felt pain like it. Every day I was falling deeper and deeper into depression. My anxiety over the past months had isolated me from the outside world. I barely left the house. I travelled to shops out of the area where I knew I wouldn't bump into anyone familiar.

I was such a confident bubbly person and loved being around people but the trauma of my marriage break up was so hard to bear that it triggered crippling anxiety attacks and deep bouts of depression. I had suffered with depression for several years due to the financial strain from running my own fitness business but I was still an extrovert in a lot of ways, loving to be out in good company but that was back in the day, before all of this changed my life. I am now the total opposite of who I was and struggle to adjust even after so many months.

Now I will take you through a fortnight in my world, a few months after it all fell apart.

It basically gives you a glimpse into my day to day thoughts, feelings and emotions.

This is how I have lived my life over the past year which left me full of self-doubt, feeling like I didn't have the strength to carry on and not even the love of my family could pull me out of my darkest days.

Constantly falling down and struggling through each and every day but I never gave up even though the journey was hard.

Day 1 (9th Jan 2017)

Wake 5am, never woke this early in months but for some reason I feel positive and ready to start my new life today! Yes, today was definitely the day when I start my road to recovery, admittedly, I tried this challenge a few weeks back but failed miserably. I had to pull myself out of the darkness and start living the life I always wanted despite my broken heart.

People separate every day, divorce is nothing new but I never ever thought that it would be something that would happen to me. All marriages have their rough patches but it seems it was

16

too rough for my husband to hold on and so he fell out of love with me and conveniently moved on with someone else.

I knew that my marriage was over, his behaviour changed, he started taking more care of his appearance, and he started to become distant. It was obvious that there was something going on, he could never look me in the eye, he was very uneasy around me and although to this day he denies that he had an affair it's clear that his dirty secret was eating him away... He looked drawn and miserable and I know it's because of his guilt. Nearly 20 years we were together and had 2 precious kids who we both adored.

When people tell you that divorce is worse than death, I believe it 100% especially when you still hold a lot of love for your husband and he has fallen in love with someone else. The total devastation and pain are beyond words. No matter what people tell you, nothing helps. It was the death of my marriage but no one had died, life carried on without him but for me it stood still. From now on my life would never ever be the same again. I was tormented by thoughts of him with her, I felt sick.

My mental health began to really spiral downwards. I didn't feel like me anymore and my episodes were becoming more frequent and very scary. I would zone out and be paralysed by a thousand thoughts, which didn't make any sense; just lots of thoughts at once like a hurricane in my

head. I couldn't focus or concentrate; it was as if something had taken over me. It wasn't me, it didn't feel like me.

I was living a nightmare.

My panic attacks became so bad that I couldn't leave the house. I couldn't work, I felt like a failure. My marriage had failed with my business to blame but I could no longer work due to my break up. It felt like I was left with nothing.

It dawned on me that I had actually lost my whole life, my husband who was also my best friend, my home, my identity, my business, my old life was gone, I even lost friends and family due to isolating myself because we had the same circle of friends, it wasn't the same without him by my side, I just couldn't put myself through it so I chose to lock myself away from everyone.

The emptiness and grief consumed me, unbearable pain that never lifted. I lost interest in everything, I just existed and the days and nights were so long. I walked around the house in a trance. I turned to food to try to fill the painful void within me, I started to comfort eat and quickly gained a huge amount of weight. I felt disgusted with myself but I couldn't stop, it took over me and because I hadn't worked out in months the weight piled on. Now I was dumped and a fat pathetic mess!

Beating myself up and falling into daily rapid cycles of highs and lows, confused and emotional. I needed to get a bloody grip.

Each day started off with me feeling positive and ready to focus on the future but thoughts of my ex soon showed their ugly face and then I felt like I had been hit by a bus. I quickly tried to change my thoughts to something else more positive but still it managed to dominate and swarm all over me.

When will I get over this heartbreak and move on with my life. I am desperate to come up for air and start living again.

Day 2

Woke at 5am again, I am going to bed earlier so I do not eat the content of the fridge every night like I have been.

I was seriously ravishing my body with comfort food and processed crap, so much so that I was scoffing down obscene amounts of chocolate every single day. Binge eating was taking over my life and it became a vicious cycle. I had to stop and take a look at my life and what I was doing on a daily basis, which was so damaging. Self-loathing, dwelling on the past, I was basically on a self-destruction journey that was making me feel even worse.

My weight rapidly increased to the point where I felt heavily pregnant, I was breathless and lethargic, hating my expanding body while my mind was poisoned with irrational thoughts.

I was in a very dark place and the thoughts that consume you are paralysing and every day has been a constant battle for me.

I self-help and educate myself as much as I can and believe that I will recover in time. I have got to hold onto that belief.

Today was another 'good' day, I have focused on changing my thought processes and I am trying so hard, believe me, I am determined to get through this. Its only day 2 but all is good.

I had my initial mental health assessment today and start therapy in 2 weeks. I have already had numerous sessions but the program ended before Christmas. I did feel better following the sessions and it is beneficial to talk to someone on the outside who can just listen and give advice and help you to see things differently.

I tell you what has helped me this week, the love and support of my family and friends; I can't thank them enough for looking out for me. I have lived in a bubble of torment for so long and zoned out, didn't feel like myself, didn't recognise myself but slowly a little bit of the old me has started to poke out of the dark clouds.... Yep I am ready for my comeback or so I thought!

Day 3

Ok so I had a little sleep in this morning after a long night of over thinking, crying and feeling sorry for myself, another self-pity party for one. I am still in disbelief that my marriage is over, I mean how long is the pain gonna stay with me, when will it dissipate?

I am only into my third day but yet again, I woke up with positive intention. As I went down the staircase there was a piece of paper on the floor at the bottom of the stairs, as I got closer I realised that it was a note from the kids. To mammy we love you xxxx, it made me gasp and I filled up with tears, tears of gratitude. That little note changed my day, I had an overwhelming feeling of love for them and realised that actually I am very lucky, I am blessed and I am going to accept my life as it is and live it because they need me and I need to be strong for them.

I have been looking forward to seeing two friends of mine today as they plan to pop over to see me. They became my first clients when I opened my fitness studio and they have been supporting me ever since.

After I locked the doors to my studio, I decided to take my boot camps outdoors in the middle of winter but there would be no overheads, I was finding it hard to put lesson plans together, my mind wasn't on the job and it wasn't fair to my clients so I abandoned my outdoor boot camp sessions around April/May I couldn't work, my life was over and my business was to blame for my marriage breakdown. For months I believed that.

My original plan for my business was to train instructors across the UK and beyond to teach my programs in their communities. The business didn't go to plan and it probably wasn't the right time for me to start but I have worked so hard and the business has taught me how to be resilient, how to never give up on your passion and that you have to believe in your ability to make your dreams a reality whatever the setbacks.

Day 4

Woke with a thumping headache but managed a workout during the course of the morning.

Randomly baked some egg and ham muffins for the first time ever, without a recipe, just whipped it all up in minutes and bunged it in the oven.... they were surprisingly scrumptious and I predict another batch being made later in the week!

Today I spent most of the day learning and educating myself with more life coaching skills and training videos. I am only on day 4 into my own personal challenge but I have an overwhelming urge of becoming a master. Bootylicious was originally created to help women feel better about themselves, love the body they're in, become more confident... all of those things and since I started this new unwanted chapter in my life where I felt that I had lost everything, I started to reflect on my ex yet again and how breaking up had hurt me so much. Out of the blue, hollowness crept back into my chest; my anxiety symptoms were creeping up on my thoughts while I was driving my mum home tonight. She came over for dinner and we scoffed a healthy salad and on the way home I collected my daughter from a friend's house.

It's unfortunate that my mum lives close to the family home where my ex still resides. We are waiting for it to sell and driving past the street where I lived still triggers crippling anxiety in me. You see that street is where I left my hopes and dreams and so many years of memories.

Tonight was tough, my mum noticed a change in me on the way home, thoughts of him consume me sometimes and I can't shake them off. I

try to change my thoughts and this is something I am still learning to do. It takes practice, daily practice which is mentally exhausting.

I returned home and when I put my son to bed my painful feelings increased. The pain grew and dominated my thoughts. Mum rang to see how I was and I told her I was fine. As the night went on, I turned to food to comfort myself. I had been healthy eating for four days into the challenge. I gave up crap. I was addicted to chocolate and would eat tons of it every single day; I neglected my body over the past months, so much and was at my heaviest ever weight.

I need to keep telling myself to keep strong and not to be too hard on myself because I am going through a life changing experience. I know that what I am trying to achieve is some task. It includes brand new daily rituals of exercise, healthy eating, positive self-talk, shifting my thought patterns, coping with my depression and anxiety, getting back into work but more importantly protecting my kids from any negative set backs.

Since the break up I have tried to make the experience as painless as possible for them. Our new home was filled with love and play time. Surprisingly I had so much more time for them than when we were living as a family with their father and the same goes for him, he spends much more quality time with them now. Yes, we are living separate lives but the double lives the kids have are positive ones to some extent. It takes time to adjust but since the split, we have followed a routine, which the kids settled into, from the start. Keeping a routine is very important and causes the least disruption, however, I had extreme anxiety attacks whenever I had to collect my boy from school, terrifying tingles and shortness of breath, numbing of my face and muscle spasms. I had to remove myself from the situation and decided that a change of school is the only way forward. My boy is a confident lad and I wasn't worried about him settling in anywhere else, for a 6 year old boy, he would walk up to teenagers in the park and join in their footie game.

My attacks were so intense that I couldn't leave the house and my ex now takes the kids to school and collects them. My son remains in the same school for now.

I am thankful that my anxiety has been under control for the past few weeks, but I haven't put myself into any situations for it to resurface. I continue to be a hermit, refuse invitations to go out, I just feel too vulnerable and I don't want to set myself back.

This challenge I set myself will help me to come out of my current situation, I hope that it will change me physically and mentally as I practice my daily rituals like my life depends on it.

Day 5

Woke at 6:30am feeling low because of last night and the fact that I missed my afternoon workout, I am determined to add it to today's set and that is exactly what I done.

I did have a tough night and lost control of my emotions but today is another day and I refuse to punish myself over it like I would any other time. I need to realise that I need to take my self-care seriously; I need to start loving myself, not punishing myself and neglecting my body with rubbish and tormented thoughts. Self-loathing is a pretty hard emotion to shake off. Your husband says he no longer loves you, you separate then you discover his relationship with someone else, you feel like utter shit, you feel unwanted, unloved, not good enough, I could go on and on. What I have learned so far in my challenge is that negative self-talk will not help me to move on, it will not do me any favours so I need to put a sock in it instead of a chocolate bar.

It takes a lot of energy to switch your thoughts over to positive ones but it is something that I practice and I am conscious of all day every day, I need to remember that I am changing my whole life around. I will fall down, I will meltdown, I will cry and I will probably want to give the whole challenge up time and time again. No matter what this experience brings me, I know for sure that I have to stick with it and give it everything.

I, like others have tried countless diet and exercise plans and programs and failed time after time. A lot of diets are a quick fix and are just not sustainable at all. I know exactly what advice to give others with regards to nutrition I'm a qualified clinical weight loss practitioner ffs yep it's true but contrary to this I struggle with my own self-motivation which is a fine example of how people do good for others but forget about themselves. I have felt extreme pressure to remain super fit and super confident but the truth is, I battled with my self-confidence, weight and appearance ever since I can remember. It's shit being a girl!

I was petrified of never feeling like me again. My depression changed me, massively! Insane Jayne.

Following a tearful night, the day has been long and then I get a call from mum telling me that the house has had an offer, another step closer to drawing a line under my past relationship. I really can't see me ever wanting to talk to that man again after the way he has hurt me. I hate him but I don't want to hate him because I am only hurting myself.

Feelings of confusion, sadness and regret began to fill my headspace. I was numb and spent the next few hours in a bit of a daze.

Is this it? Does this mean closure?

Day 6

Deep in the darkness - Today I spent all day eating, sleeping and crying, I don't want to wake up another day to go through this yet again. Kids are at their dads all weekend so instead of planning something and keeping myself busy, it all turns to mush and so do I.

I locked myself away from the world.

Day 7

Alone for the second day, I don't want to be miserable in front of anyone, I don't want to connect with anyone, I want to isolate myself and fall deeper into depression and self-loathing. Yeah, who wouldn't want to feel this way? It's something that I cannot switch off. I am in 'the negative zone' it's a horrible place to be, where my mind thinks of a thousand reasons not to be here, a thousand reasons why people would be better off without me, why I should end the misery. I would never attempt to end my life, I just wanted to end the pain and I found myself wishing that I wouldn't wake up.

I had so much to live for, my god I am only getting a divorce! People go through this shit every day; my husband went off with someone, big deal! That shit happens and other people don't lose the plot so why have I gone into total meltdown? Why am I suffering from the thoughts in my head, why do I feel like my heart has been ripped out of my chest? Why does it feel like I am mourning a death?

The fact of the matter is, for months, I probably didn't accept the situation I was in, nearly a year has passed so why has it taken this long to fall to pieces? Why does it feel so raw? I feel like I am suffocating, I feel like I have lost the real me and will never find her again? I blame him for this pain, I adored him and I am left devastated while he cracks on with life and a new relationship on his own doorstep! I need to stop this hatred and just let it be. I spend hours listening to self-help videos, affirmations and mediations because I want this all to end. I have a life to live so why am I not living it?

Get a grip Jayne!

Day 8

Weekend from hell but I am curled up still isolated and feeling like crap! I have wallowed in self-pity and eaten my bodyweight in chocolate and ice cream because for some reason, it comforts me until I feel sick and disgusted, I could actually list a million feelings (all of which are bad).

I battle through another day, detached from everyone and everything. I find comfort in food so I binge on shite all day long, I know what I am trying to do, I am trying to fill the emptiness I feel but instead of filling the void, it leads to feelings of shame. I am rapidly expanding and I even struggle to get up from the chair, I am literally turning into a teletubby! It's just my luck that unlike most heartbreak diets where women often lose pounds because they can't bring themselves to eat, I done the complete opposite and my binge eating became a coping mechanism and a new addiction, one that I couldn't shake off. Something had to be done before I turned into ten ton Tess.

Day 9

Something in me changes today, I think it was the fact that I weighed myself and was tipping 14 stone (how the hell did that happen)? This is a shock to me, as I have never weighed so much! So here I am, recovering from a marriage break up and looming divorce, feeling rejected, unloved, and chubs to boot! Great (rolling eyes emoji). How will I ever feel confident to leave this house again?

My anxiety is definitely something that comes into play when it's time to step out of the front door. Panic attacks have begun to lessen, but the feeling of hopelessness still remains. However, as the day progresses, I start to think more clearly and decide that from this day on, I am going to continue with my challenge despite the setbacks. I am only human after all and I have a personal goal to achieve and I am bloody well gonna get off my arse and complete it, whatever it takes... its only day 9 and already I have fallen at the first hurdle and hidden away from reality for 4 days!

What the fuck?

What a waste, so because of my relapse, I have had to input four days' worth of my journal at once..... Taking myself back to those feelings but thankfully feeling like I am in a better frame of mind for getting them out onto paper.

I was surrounded by my children and my mum today and it felt magic. My poor babies don't have any idea of the torment their mother has endured over the months. My daughter has witnessed a couple of really bad panic attacks, she has listened to my cries of heartbreak but as much as I try to keep it together, I collapse in a heap on the odd occasion. I apologise for loosing control, I am hurting like hell, I have never felt hurt like it before, it overwhelms me at times and I just crumble. I pray that she would never ever have to suffer this kind of pain.

I consider my 'old self' to be positive, very ambitious, outgoing and bubbly. I loved to make people feel good about themselves, I loved to make people laugh and I loved to laugh, it's my favourite pastime. Laughing has been fake now for a long time. The reality of my unknown future is something that terrifies me. I am 40 years old but I feel like a child, I need my mums touch, my mum's reassurance and she never fails to be there for me. It hurts me knowing that I hurt her with my inner conflict, I try so hard not to upset my mum, I don't want to upset anyone with my own battles but she can see that I am struggling, she knows when I am not me, she knows when I am in a state of depression. I can't let this define me but the longer this illness takes a hold of me, the more desperate I become and wonder when or if I will ever recover?

Day 10

Today is the day where I will intentionally be more positive; I will pull myself out of my low moods. I told myself that today is another opportunity to make a difference, to take further steps to where I want to be.

I feel like I should also shake up my exercise challenge and push hard to shift this weight. So I will do what I do best.... Bootylicious Bootcamps!

It's time to get back in the game, to find the courage to get back up on my feet and make it happen. I have had months of heartache and would hold the world record for feeling every emotion there is in a single day.

I continue to listen to inspirational stories and the realisation that I am not alone suffering from mental illness helps me along the way. All I read or hear is that time will heal, bad times will pass and I believe that until I fall back yet again. Some days I think, have I turned a corner today? Is the worst over? I keep telling myself that I will cope with whatever is thrown at me and rock bottom has given me the opportunity to reflect. I had to deal with feelings I wanted to run from. I have felt every one of them and faced them head on.

Mental illness is unpredictable, it can take over you in an instant, it can ride through you like a wave or it can stick with you like a dark shadow for days, weeks or months. Last weekend had to be the last time that I would isolate myself, I will make every effort to get out into the fresh air, visit friends and family and start feeling something other than broken. It's time to become unbroken, it's time to appreciate what is around me and get some sense of wellbeing and hope that I will come out of this nightmare a stronger happier version of me.

For those who have not experienced major depression, I wouldn't wish it on anyone, it's not being sad or unhappy, it's feelings of utter despair, worthlessness, hopelessness, self-loathing, it's the devil in you. You can barely get out of bed some days and you become caged in by your surroundings. Your mind is telling you how pathetic you are, how you are a failure and you have no purpose. That people will be better off without you, others have bigger problems than you so man the fuck up. You want to hide away from the world, which is just too hard to live in. Confused and numb with nothing to look forward to and no interest in anything at all. For me, depression changed me, it has stripped me back and I have experienced every raw emotion possible. Sometimes I don't want to wake up because I don't want to feel the excruciating pain it causes me. I would choose childbirth over heartbreak any day of the week.

It's easy for people to judge, before I started suffering with anxiety I really could not understand how someone could not leave their own house, they couldn't go out in fear of something really bad happening, something actually happening in that moment. Anxiety makes you fearful that something bad is going to happen, you are convinced of it, which leads you to avoid certain situations.

Its midday and the morning workout I promised myself I would do hasn't happened yet! I am worried that my true fitness levels will be exposed since my last boot camp workout was around 9 months ago!

I need to remember that I am starting as a beginner all over again, overweight, tired and a bit scared of collapsing from exhaustion truth be known! These boot camps aren't easy, but I plough my way through every set, wishing the counter would hurry the fuck up as I start to get heartburn and acid reflux, my joints start aching and the sweat pours down my back, Jesus, call me an ambulance!

Finally I complete the last set and walk around the lounge with my hands in the air as if I just won a gold medal at the Olympics! I kid you not I was a champ! How I have missed that feeling of accomplishment following a brutal workout. Yes! My first boot camp done and dusted – Whoop! It felt great, the endorphins didn't know what to do with themselves but I won't forget my first victory and the positive energy it gave me even if the buzz was for only a few minutes, it's a start.

When I say that I am a beginner it's no lie. I have huge respect for people trying to shift a hell of a lot of weight, being this heavy has caused a lot of health issues for me and I now know what it feels like to

work out on the opposite spectrum, it really is so much harder and it makes me feel I am a little overwhelmed at the journey ahead of me and I know it will be far from easy but if I stick with my rituals from this day forth, I will conquer my demons, slim down my body frame and hopefully fix my broken mindset, day by day, step by step.

The smallest of tasks feel impossible, so for me, waking up, making the bed, sorting the laundry and washing pots is quite an achievement. Something that is automatic or second nature for many is literally a job in itself for sufferers of depression.

I jump in the shower and get ready for a meeting I arranged with a guy who practices visualisation techniques. I am keen to include it in this challenge to see what results I get. High vibrational thinking.

I put on some make up and it made me feel better. I rarely look in the mirror because I hate what is looking back at me. I rarely get dressed unless I need to go to the shop. My life now is so much different than it was when I was married and working. I miss the old me, from way back, before the depression and stress turned my world upside down.

I squeeze into my clothes because I refuse to accept that I am 4 stone heavier! Did I say that out loud? Massive gulp! Seriously though, I have been such a mess and my medication states that a side effect is a ferocious appetite (are you kidding me!) I gained around a stone in my first week and swiftly went back to the doctor saying that I will never feel well if I am gaining weight so rapidly, I have struggled all my life with body issues and low self-esteem so how on earth is gaining shed loads of lard going to cure my depression? I am now obese and feeling depressed about that too!

I have made an effort to give myself positive self-talk today and although I am repulsed by my expanding body, I try to feel grateful for my big booty and I have the ability to workout and that people actually pay money to get a set of boobs the size of mine.

I make a decision to start to love myself again as I get into my body transformation zone. I will reward myself with things I want, new (smaller) clothes for starters. No more junk food binges, I cannot put my body through that anymore. I need loving care and attention and I will learn to love what I have and keep improving myself until I reach my target weight.

Following my meeting with Steve who has studied High Vibrational Thinking and published many books on the subject, I felt like the penny dropped about the negative energy that we carry within us. Your thoughts become your reality so when you are feeling pain and anger, thinking of what happened that created these feelings will only feed the negative energy and charge it up like a battery. Once you get an understanding of this, you can put techniques into place to help you to consciously change your thought patterns that will result in a happier life. Think happy - be happy. Think sad then you will be sad. I have been feeding my negative energy for months without realising the damage it was causing me.

I never want to fall into depression like that again. I starting reading a book Steve sent me regarding relationships and the reasons why we break up and fall out of love and it also covers the relationship you have with your children. It was a reality check that I needed to change my situation and focus on my recovery for the sake of them. My battle with depression and anxiety and the effect my marriage break up had on my thoughts was like an evil demon taking over my body, I wanted never to wake up to face another day. The last episode I had was the last one. I had to change my life and practice conscious thinking and change my thought processes.

Day 11

So it's taken me this long to suddenly realise that everything I was doing in my quest for self help and recovery was not really having the desired effect. I have been taking another kind of antidepressants for a couple of months and I had my worst suicidal episode ever last weekend (how can that happen?) Unfortunately antidepressants only mask the problem they don't actually solve it. I found myself watching videos on thoughts of suicide and although I would never attempt to take my own life, as I said before but the demon inside me would have handed me the pills!

I have spent months, reading about how to overcome divorce, how to change your life, how to be happy, how to deal with anxiety etc. I have pretty much researched every subject and I am starting a new therapy program next week to help me to deal with this nightmare life transition I have no choice but to endure. I figured out that it is what it is and for me to progress positively, I had to make the necessary changes to my everyday thinking.

I have learned heaps along the way and what hasn't worked for me in the past will not work in the future, I have discovered this the hard way and now I was paying the price. It's time to recondition my thinking.

My choices in life were never meant for me to end up a divorced mother of two with a mental illness and having to rebuild my life all over again at the age of 40! You know your relationship is suffering but whatever you do seems to be the wrong decision and I can't believe it's been nearly a year since we separated and I moved out. It's taken me so long to get some stability in my life.

I have now put into practice to consciously think about my every thought and any negativity that tries to take over my headspace will get a kick up the arse and sent on its way.

I made the beds, done more washing and cooked spaghetti bolognaise and cottage pie. It's the first day in 9 months that hasn't dragged me to the floor and I have had no time to think negative thoughts. I even received a text from the ex about the divorce and settlement. If I had received it last week I would

40

of text back angrily with CAPITAL LETTERS but instead, I calmly read the content and responded with a 'forgive you message'.

I feel like I have regained the power back as well as control over my emotions and I will repeat it all again one day at a time until it becomes second nature, however, before I get over excited about the progress made so far from this new approach I will see how tomorrow pans out so chow for now!

Oh yeah nearly forgot to mention my 2nd victory in the Bootylicious boot camps challenge which has left my body aching (you know the type of aching' it is so painful it makes you laugh but also want to cry taking every step) The good thing about my achy limbs is that it's the result of blood sweat and tears, it's the proof to myself that I have actually accomplished another brutal workout so why am I still fat!?

Day 12

These early morning get ups are a breeze. I listen to a morning meditation before I face the day. I am going to tackle the challenge from now on from another perspective.

OK so following the piss poor attempt of 'my new life new me challenge', which left me feeling even worse than ever, I knew there must be something that will switch my focus and ability to stick with a plan and see it through.

It was time to forget all past attempts, which I repeated and continued to fail time after time. None of them were sustainable which resulted in me gaining more weight than ever! It's time for radical change.

I met with Steve again who manages to make me feel better the 'High Vibrational Thinking' guy. He teaches me how to live a more fulfilling and happier life that was free from stress and negativity. Who wouldn't want to live in a world like that, all unicorns and rainbows?

I left his house feeling more focused and ready to try and implement what he suggested into my day-to-day life. I started to try and meditate from You Tube videos but I couldn't seem to take it all in and I just gave up but I was determined to keep trying other techniques. For me, talking about my feelings to someone who will listen helped me to have a better understanding of what feelings I was experiencing and how I could help myself to let the past go and move on with my life.

I told him that my weekend was one of my worst episodes and I felt so desperate never to return to that dark place again. All the positive affirmations, motivational videos and quotes did help me for a short period of time then something would just

42

knock me back and the negativity just crept back into my thoughts and I was unable to tap into a positive mindset.

Steve talked through and explained the techniques again and it was like something clicked. I left feeling much more determined and focused than I had felt for months. I literally could not believe how different I felt and I started to experience more positive feelings about achieving my challenge and coming out of the transformation a better version of me.

I realised that the reason people don't stick to a plan or continue to make the same mistakes over and over again when taking on a new health and weight loss challenge is that you go into the plan with the same old mindset. You dread the challenge and it feels like a punishment and concentrating on all the negative aspects like restricting yourself with rules and cutting out the foods you love - takes away everything that you enjoy. It leaves you feeling beat before you even start. No alcohol, no chocolate, no sugar no carbs. Your mindset is the NO ZONE.

It's pretty simple, change the way you see the challenge ahead and you will change your results. Instead of telling yourself, you have so much weight to lose, you are so unfit, you are fat etc. try and switch the negative self-talk and start saying to yourself, I can do this, I am going to succeed, I love my body I am improving my life and I will feel amazing when the challenge is done. You must be consciously thinking every minute about the thoughts that enter your head in any given situation. Everything is made of energy and all energy vibrates at a frequency, happy people are vibrating at a fast positive vibration and sad, angry depressed people are vibrating at a slow more negative vibration.

We all have a 'devil' inside of us (which is negative energy, you could call it trapped emotional negative energy) and when something happens to upset us and we feel bad this feeds it with more thoughts of negativity allowing it to become more powerful and in control.

If you imagine the energy as an object and visualise it, this helps you to identify it when it takes over your thought processes. Once you realise that a thought is negative, you have to deliberately change your thoughts to something else so as not to feed it. It really does work but you have to stick with it, rinse and repeat.

What you think you receive, what you give out you will get back so stop any negative thinking NOW and start to practice living a positive life. Once you change your thinking, positive experiences and things come to you and your life will become noticeably better. BUT it will not stay that way if you do not put the work into rewiring your mindset, commit to take up the challenge and keep a journal of each day.

You can apply this technique to anything. If you feel angry about something, acknowledge how it makes you feel but switch the thought to something positive, something that makes you feel good, you will soon raise your vibration and then you will attract experiences with more high vibrational energies such as love, hope and happiness etc.

Imagine that you will complete the challenge successfully and the techniques you are introducing to your current schedule will guarantee a better outcome then any previous attempts. You must start to think about things in a different way to make it become a habit that will benefit your overall wellbeing and outlook on life and situations.

If something angers you, take a few deep breaths and think about the outcome if you were to kick off about it, is it really worth getting yourself upset over? If you think about the real problems in the world you will know that it is trivial and not worth giving it any more attention. It's human nature due to the negative energy that we all have trapped within us to moan and groan about things that we think are important to us but if you look at it from another angle, you will start to push out irrelevant negative thoughts and stop feeding the negativity within and soon you will be free from it.

Day 13 – A DAY OUT!

I actually cannot believe the change in me today. Just one week ago I was wishing I wasn't here, the lowest I have ever felt, me feeling ok was honestly not ok but I was getting through the long days as best I could. It was like the life was sucked out of me, depression had really taken over my being and there was no fight left, well so I thought.

This morning I listened to some meditation and jumped out of bed pumped up for a morning workout, it energises me and it sets me on the right path to face the day.

It's my weekend to have the kids and it's Saturday morning, I planned to take them to the cinema, it was our first day out in months, due to my crippling anxiety and depression, I was unable to go out but today I felt different, the fear was gone as if by magic!

I was filled with positive energy and excitement and the kids came back from their dads and the energy in the house was so much different than it had been. I remember reading that when you change your thinking and recognise your feelings, you can become happy and your life will just change, good things will happen, love will be drawn to you and opportunities will arise. I was looking for signs that this was true and I got them.

The cinema was showing the movie Sing, it was an animated film about all creatures, an X Factor audition style movie but for animals. The first sign I received was the Beyoncé soundtrack which started at the beginning of the movie, Bootylicious was the connection but that was just a coincidence right? Then the koala said 'when you hit rock bottom, the only way is up' The movie was basically about following your dreams and believing that you can do whatever you put your mind to. Another character of the movie was an Elephant, she wanted to audition so badly but the fear she felt prevented her and she ended up missing out on the big audition day. Later she returned to the theatre to ask for another chance and without giving you a full commentary of the movie, she had an incredible voice and she performed with a standing ovation and it all ended well, like most movies do. So I started to believe that this movie was showing me the signs I needed to get back in the game and follow my dreams. Sometimes it's subtle signs like this that can get you right back on track.

Driving home, there was an advertising board with the words DREAM facing the dual carriageway.

Not only did the penny drop but I started to see positive things, positive signs that I would never have noticed while I was in my depressive state of mind. You can't see the woods for the trees so they say. It does take some practice and you find yourself thinking about your thoughts constantly but this is what you must do to make the change.

The next obstacle to overcome was to make peace with my ex, he was my children's father after all and whatever he does from now cannot and will not affect me anymore!

The past is gone but it was time to forgive and move on. This is something that takes time to master because we are all programmed to live a certain way, influences from the people who we are surrounded by, our upbringings and past events all play a part in the life we live today. Training yourself to do something different than

what you are used to is a difficult task but it's the only way to change the way you live and the outcome.

I had been so unwell that I couldn't take the kids anywhere, I struggled for months but I had to make a change and start living my life again.

Day 14

An old school friend of mine text me last night to say she was coming to visit. I was so excited to see her but I started feeling anxious about her coming over. I was doing so well keeping my depression at bay and I didn't want it to resurface because I knew that we would be discussing what had happened. I cancelled, I sent a text to say I had work to do (which wasn't a lie) I did have stuff to do but the real reason was that I just wasn't ready to talk about it or see anyone. I need to keep my focus on my personal development.

A new therapy program starts today and when I was explaining how far I had come from last weekend (the weekend when I wanted to give up) to the weekend just gone when I took the kids to the cinema and had a day out full of fun and family time, I had to stop and think 'is this really me'?

I cried happy tears at the fact that I had come so far from my darkest days - I mean this is serious shit I am talking about, the shit everyone takes for granted... Going out for the day without panic, without doubt, without a care in the world...

I felt a bit drained following the session, it brings up the raw emotions that I have tried to keep a lid on and the goal I have set myself is pretty magnificent! I am literally starting a brand new life, the new me is in progress, the old me is the past and

I'm saying goodbye forever and chasing the person who I always wanted to be, the new me who has found the courage and strength to make something of her life, to enjoy her journey and to trust that the path she is taking is the right one.

In life you have two choices, you walk the path of fear, hate, depression and all the nasty negative feelings and emotions that come with it or you walk the path of love, compassion and abundance where there is laughter, fun and opportunities.

We choose the life we want, no-one else and if there is one thing that I have learned from the most devastating experience in life it is that no matter how much we hurt, the pain will pass, no matter how bad things get they will always get better. Nothing stays the same and we have to deal with the changes that come along and make the most of them. When something ends, it means a new beginning and so here it is.

It is the week of my wedding anniversary and this time last year I was unaware of who my husband was seeing, I even had hopes that we could find our way back together eventually. When you spend so many years with someone, for him or her to leave you for someone else is another level of devastation. Your mind goes into over drive, you start piecing everything together, all the secrets and lies and it eats away at you.

I am still tormented some days with sadness and hurt. I can control my thoughts a little better committing myself to learning more about psychology of the mind and dealing with emotions and feelings have given me a better understanding of what I was living through and how to take things from a different perspective.

When someone hurts me I get angry, projecting my pain with vicious words, that is how I dealt with past anger, before I had an understanding of how I could control my emotions and not let anyone affect me. Only I could allow myself to feel hurt from my own destructive thoughts. Thoughts become feelings and through months of self-development and research, I began to manage my thoughts in a much healthier way. This is not an easy task and takes considerable discipline.

Divorce is far from funny and some people may think that neither am I but that's how I cope, just take the piss out of the situation and try to see the bright side.

I mean lets face it; I am free to do what I want, to live a Shirley Valentine lifestyle if I wanted to. To go where I want with whomever I want.

I struggled to come to terms with everything and I only had two choices, let it define me and be stuck forever in the dark full of anger and resentment or do I scrape myself off the floor and fight my way to a happy future?

What I was facing was inevitable; my husband had fallen out of love with me into the arms of another.

Looking back now, I can see why I fell into deep despair, my marriage fell apart at around the same time I lost my fitness studio - I carried on regardless on autopilot, trying to build my empire and support my children the best way I could.

The breakup took its toll and a few months living in a new home with the kids, I had to stop working. You can never prepare yourself for your husband moving on with someone else when you loved him so much. Yes we had problems but you make a marriage work but instead I feel he gave up on us... For better or worse? It's too easy for people these days to go off with someone else, no one fights for marriage anymore and that's a shame.

I honestly don't know how I survived it but I am here now to tell you my story and hope to help others going through the same.

You hear and read about divorce every day but never could you imagine the raw pain and despair it actually causes to personally go through it yourself with 2 kids and when you have been with your husband nearly 20 years! Being a wife and mother was so important to me but when I had a desire to start my own business, I never ever expected my life to fall apart a few years later so tragically.

I was mourning the death of my marriage and I could not function. I isolated myself from the world and I could not cope with the grief I felt it hurt so much the void in my chest consumed me and it stayed with me to the point of me not giving a damn if I woke up to face another day. I just wanted the pain to stop, my thoughts took over and the anger I felt changed me into someone I didn't recognise anymore.

No one really knew the extent of my condition apart from my closest friends and my mum, it destroyed me and it was hurting my mum which made me feel worse but I couldn't snap out of it. I was zoned out most days, not making sense of anything and not thinking straight. The anxiety for me was harder to deal with because it prevented me from even collecting my son from school, I couldn't return because the thought of bumping into people just filled me with dread, driving past the street where I lived was a major trigger.

I spent months researching and understanding what was happening to me and all I wanted was to feel like me again and stop this distress. I have never felt so lonely and vulnerable in my life. I was convinced no one gave a damn and I was fighting my own battle.

I contacted my doctor because my thoughts were becoming worrying, I felt doomed, I felt worthless, I felt unwanted, a massive failure. I couldn't see any light at the end of the tunnel, nothing interested me and I didn't want the kids to see their mum so dysfunctional.

Chapter Four: Ibiza with my bestie

Although my mum was by my side throughout every meltdown and every tear I didn't want to worry her more than I already did and I was lucky that my bestie provided consistent love and support on a daily basis, even though she was running her super successful business, she always took the time to contact me every day.

We started going to business events together and attended a training course, which got me out of the house, back into normality with something else to focus on. At this stage, the realisation of what I was going through never hit me. I was adjusting to the fact that my life would change forever. I lost my personality while I was unwell; I lost myself and couldn't concentrate on anything.

We started eating out and getting merry on the vino, which was great until I would get upset and spoil the night. I lay awake crying most nights, I was trying so hard to enjoy myself but I was dark behind the eyes and I felt empty. I would be laughing one minute and bursting into tears the next.

A few months before, we had planned to take the kids over to Spain to visit my dad. The kids loved it, she also has a son and daughter and we all had a great time.

I began to plan getting back into business mode and try to turn my life around. I had spent months cut off from the world, my family, friends and social media.

We buzzed off each other and built each other up, I was so proud of her achievements and she was so strong and resilient, she had been betrayed herself and came through it fighting. Nothing will keep her down.

I remember when I started to look forward to the future again, I found the confidence to go out more and while we were sat in a local pub on a quiet Wednesday evening (my kids were with their dad) her phone rang. It was a man who we had met a couple of times a few months back and we all got on really well, he invited her and a friend to join him on holiday at his sons luxury villa in Ibiza! He recently split from his girlfriend who he planned to take but didn't want to go alone. We jumped at the opportunity but didn't really take it in. We booked our flights and were excited but a little unsure that this was actually real. It was just what I needed, to get away from everything and get my head together. We started getting sugar daddy comments about going away with him but it was nothing like that, he invited others too and was just a kind man who thought we deserved a break.

After the most awful year, I needed this trip more than anything. To get away from reality and chill out and that was exactly what we did but this was on another level.

Once we arrived at the Villa, the gates opened and behind it stood the most epic villa I had ever seen. It was seriously overwhelming, nothing at all what we expected and I actually cried when I realised we were staying there for 7 nights - unreal!

This villa was something a celebrity would rent; it was amazing, accommodating 12 people and had a view of Ibiza Town with beautiful landscaped grounds, private pool, outdoor dining area, and hot tub room to seat 20 people with a very high end specification throughout. (I sounded like an estate agent for a minute)

It took a couple of days to actually take it all in, talk about paradise, we were in it!

That holiday literally changed my life. The second day in, I was taking a swim in the pool and suddenly an idea came into my head. I had always believed that my business would be a success one day and that I would never give up on it, especially now that my husband had well and truly moved on.

Admittedly, I have had so many ideas for the business and that was where I failed, I tried too many things at once to try to make ends meet and to prove to my husband that it would all come good in the end and we would live an incredible lifestyle.

Some people may think that I chose my business over my husband but that was not the case at all. I worked my arse off and never gave up building a better life for my family. My husband couldn't see my vision and obviously felt pushed out. My business got the blame.

I have more reason than ever to get back into the zone and provide my kids with the best life possible. My dreams were big and most people probably thought I was deluded but there was no way I would give up after working so hard.

So back to the holiday.... I was taking a swim and there it was the best idea yet. I called the agent who managed the villa regarding winter fees and started researching retreats in Ibiza. That was it; I was going to put my heart and soul into creating a program to help divorced women. Bootylicious was going the get a facelift and make the comeback of all comebacks!

I literally planned the whole retreat while I still enjoyed the sun and in such beautiful surroundings I had a taste of the good life and wanted more.

I believe I was at the villa for a reason and it wasn't only this that made me feel sure that this was the direction to take.

The day before we left to return home, we went to Ocean Beach (opening party) it was literally the best party ever and we had a blast, however, the most bizarre thing happened.

As I left the ladies I recognised a face in the queue... Shelly is that you? She looked at me with hesitation, it's me Jayne 'Bootylicious' - Let me tell you the story about my (choreographer).

When I started Bootylicious Boot camps around 5 years ago, I created a very sassy and sexy workout that was to help women feel confident about their body no matter what their shape or size.

Miss Booty Workout was launched and we trained instructors nationwide in Teesside and Manchester. The workout was awesome but unbeknown to me there would be drastic consequences. I signed up for a 2-year lease on a building that I planned to use as a fitness studio.

The pressure of trying to establish the studio and the financial obligations that come with it meant I was unable to continue with Miss Booty and had to shelve it until I was in a position to fire it up again.

During this time an amazing choreographer from the south connected with me while I was promoting the workout across the country and she was perfect for the job. I didn't want to be the face of the workout, I wanted to run things behind the scenes but she was perfect for the brand. We had been planning to meet up for over 3 years but busy schedules prevented us meeting up until now! In Ibiza of all the places (yes another sign that proved I was meant to focus on my new plans and stick with them) It reignited my passion and I was convinced that these were all signs about a potentially much brighter future.

We were both gob smacked to say the least, this was unbelievable, after all this time we finally met.

I mentioned my new plans for the business and she was delighted at the idea of a new opportunity, she always believed in the concept, she got it and I was certain that we would work together at some point.

Even though I was enjoying the holiday I really missed the kids, I had never left them before but I needed to get away from a life that became unbearable at times.

The day after my return from Ibiza, my right foot became swollen and I could barely walk on it. I went to A&E where they diagnosed cellulitis - I came home with antibiotics and pain relief but nothing took away the pain. I was in agony! I planned to start my daily exercise routine as soon as I arrived back from my trip because my weight was still a real issue to me. Although Bootylicious represented all women, I still had my own debilitating insecurities and had never been so overweight; I felt I was in the wrong body.

The first thing you would think is that I fell over drunk and damaged my foot but the only thing I can connect my injury to was that as I got into the back of a taxi which was taking us to the airport to come home on our last day, I felt a cramp for a few seconds, I walked across the airport, through baggage departures and drove back home which was an hours journey. I wasn't in any pain at all so you can imagine my concerns when I woke up the next day with it swollen.

I returned to the hospital and they gave me an X-ray the results came back and I was informed that I had fractured my foot! I couldn't believe it at all but the pain was so bad that I had to go upstairs on my hands and knees.

With the discovery of the news I thought to myself that all I want is to be happy and healthy, yet another setback as my positive plans now had a black cloud over them. I was advised to wear a moon boot and to return 4 weeks later; however, they said they might need to operate! Are they having a giraffe?

This was pulling me back into depression but tried my hardest to remain upbeat despite the fact that I couldn't leave the house (yet again) this time for other reasons but my condition escalated again with frustration.

Sure enough, my depression and anxiety returned on a massive scale and my mental health began to decline again. Over thinking was a specialty of mine and I had a very good knack at tormenting myself with negative thoughts. It was like a poison.

Determined to get my head right, I jumped on the internet to self- educate on self-coaching and how to help others and the best exercises to do with a knackered foot.

The initial focus was to finish this book that will generate an income and most importantly, change lives. I know for sure that this is what is needed to step into the future and start earning.

Writing down my thoughts became a daily activity.

Chapter Five: School holidays and a new family member

It's been tough living through the past months but now that my foot is healing well, I am looking forward to getting about more and I have lots planned for over the holidays.

The kids are going away with their dad; it will be their first holiday without me. I remember how I felt taking them last year without him; I was still in denial at this point, in disbelief that I was living life without him after so many years together.

Watching other families sharing fun times and making memories was difficult. I felt lost, but I made the most of it for the sake of the kids. I wanted them to experience a better life with more quality time together.

It all feels like a distant memory, I only remember bits while I made the transition from my old life. Adjusting to living without my husband was extremely difficult and even now the pain hits me out of the blue.

Today is the day of the first family holiday without me, I wonder how it feels for them, and I wonder if he thinks of me and the memories from other holidays that we shared together.

It's these moments for me, when I am with my children, doing the things that we all did as a family, it's these moments that cut like a knife. We are living as a 'broken' family, no longer together and every new adventure will never be quite the same again.

My boy sobbed his heart out as he hugged me goodbye, I was fine up until that point. I had made heaps of plans to keep myself busy because I knew that a week without them would have a detrimental effect on my condition. My mum was on hand every day to help me like she always is and after a good cry and lots of hugs with her I knew that I would be fine.

The kids are having a great time, I have been receiving texts videos and photographs from them having fun and it's such a relief that they are enjoying themselves.

While the kids are away I set myself a deadline to finish my book and write until I had completed a draft. I have only just started to work on it a little every day because I feel strong enough to revisit the events of the past year that had ruined me. Something keeps pulling me towards this book and little signs were appearing which made me realise that this had to be done.

It's day 2 of the kids holiday and I have been keeping myself busy, my to do list was shrinking and a productive day made me feel in good form, however, that all came crashing down when Layla came dashing in from the garden yelping from a wasp sting.... I had a panic attack, Layla was our new addition to the family, I kept pressing the wrong number to call someone and help. I managed to get her to the vet where they confirmed it was a sting in her mouth, my poor little pup. I felt so guilty but my reaction to it all proved that my panic attacks weren't a thing of the past like I hoped.

My anxiety had increased from going 'cold turkey' on my medication that I prepared myself for but I felt out of control when she was crying in pain. I thought the worst; the kids were away and if anything would have happened to her it would devastate me.

I have tried so hard to get myself well and start living life again but it seems that the progress is slow and the setbacks just keep on coming.

The truth is that obstacles and setbacks are part of life. I have to carry on and know in my heart that things will get better. Changing negative emotions when things go wrong is a hard habit to break. Mindset is everything; the decisions you make will become the blueprint of your life. It's time I stepped up my game and focused on the good and only the good.

As the weeks go by I practice more on switching my thoughts and saying positive affirmations to myself (these pep talks are crucial) Reminding myself that I am strong, I am enough and I can do this...

Visualisation became second nature to me and at every opportunity I would imagine my life as I wanted it to be, day dreaming and connecting with the emotion of how it feels to be my future self, it's a proven method to get you closer to living the life you want and I was focused on getting there.

At first you may feel a little unsure about talking to yourself but you need to treat yourself like you would a family member or friend, you would encourage them so why not be your own advocate?

Within a week I was feeling so much better, my puppy alarm clock aka Layla was the wakeup call I needed to get out of bed and start my day... at 5:30am! This took some time to adjust and early afternoons would hit me with fatigue but by 10am I felt like I had done heaps of super productive work and it mentally set me up for the day ahead. My bedtime routine started at 10pm where I would listen to YouTube on anything that would be beneficial to my personal growth. Reflecting on the day and expressing gratitude for everything I have.

Chapter Six: Depression for me

I know that people meant well telling me that I have two beautiful children to live for, I was aware of this but I felt a burden to them, like they would be better off without me.

I remember one of the most terrifying moments when I had enough of the day, it seemed to go on forever, the pain in my chest was unbearable, I just wanted to go to bed early and hopefully wake up feeling better the next day.

My son was with his dad and my mum took my daughter home with her so I could go to bed. It was 6pm and I took some sleeping pills in the hope that I would go to sleep soon after, how wrong was I. I spent the next few hours tossing and turning in bed with my heart pounding out of my chest, anxiety was through the roof, it became that bad that I went downstairs and faced the wall in the dark rocking back and forth thinking to myself that I wanted to die, I didn't want to wake up and go through another day of the pain that was suffocating me.

I called my mum in tears and said that I need help, I need to go to the hospital, and I could no longer go on. She called a taxi but arrived with my daughter.... in tears I said that she couldn't see me like this; it must have been horrifying for her to witness. I felt such a failure, I lost everything and now I couldn't even look after my own kids, I was such a mess. I hugged her and said I am so sorry, don't be frightened, I am not your mam at the moment, this isn't me it's my illness, I will get better I promise. She has kept it together and been so understanding helping me through some really difficult days, especially through my panic attacks, they struck at any moment, recurring daily at one point - She kept me calm and stayed with me making me feel safe. Going through it has made us closer and I love spending time with her, real quality time.

You have to treat depression like you would any other illness. You need to rest but you also need to distract yourself from your demeaning thoughts. This is not easy, these negative thoughts multiply and you find yourself in a world of self-loathing, doubt, anger and despair and you see no way out.

If I had a job to go out to I know that I wouldn't have become so seriously ill. My confidence was ripped from me, I couldn't continue to teach boot camps and shut myself off from the world outside, this was the worst thing that I could have done and it was feeding my depression.

I could barely leave the house seriously, you have lived your life up to this point, in autopilot and suddenly you are numb and too afraid to step outside.

Some may not understand how I could have become so ill over losing the love of my husband to someone else but I married him 'forever' even through hard times I never imagined life without him. For someone you cared for so much to hurt you like that is probably going to sting for the rest of your life, It's a betrayal that cannot be forgotten but you have to forgive for you own peace but it will never go away, you just have to bury it and get on with your life.

I was never really a spiritual person until I hit rock bottom. I was so out of my depth with my circumstances but I wanted to find out the reasons I was feeling so overwhelmed, confused and uncertain if I would ever be well again.

During the toughest days when I couldn't get out of bed, I lay for hours, I was suffering, really suffering and my mind was replaying the same thoughts over and over again. The anger and rage I felt consumed me and I was so scared to face the day.

I have learnt not to be too hard on myself, stop blaming myself and just take care of my body and mind.

So here I am, finally confident with my life moving forward and ready for a new chapter.

Implementing positive changes and sticking with them was the key to my success and now I am ready .for my comeback... I am still a work in progress but I will always learn and develop to live a life of abundance.

I now know what happened in my life was meant for me, the pain and suffering was meant for me, everything was building my pathway to creating a better life. A more fulfilling life with hope and purpose.

I just couldn't seem to stop negative thoughts from creeping in, every single day there were thoughts of my past and I thought I would never be free from the hurt inside.

The good news is that every day is one step further to fully recovering from the personal trauma that I went through. There will always be bad days and I accept that and looking from other perspectives now helps me to release the negative emotions in a positive way, slowly over time the hate dissolves as I reach the acceptance stage of the grief cycle.

So what is the grief cycle?

It's the same emotional rollercoaster that you experience from the death or loss of a loved one. It was the death of my marriage and the devastating loss of my husband. It is a cycle of different stages.

Stage 1 – Denial and isolation

At the initial shock of hearing my husband respond (no) when I asked him if he loved me. He told me that he didn't want to hurt me! The only thing I wanted to do was run away and never come back. I couldn't stay where I wasn't wanted. This was my way of dealing with the situation and I fled the home we shared for so long.

Stage 2 – Anger

Once the reality kicked in I had an explosion of anger and resentment, which ran through my body, I couldn't believe that he fell out of love with me after everything we had been through.

Stage 3 – Bargaining

You can't make someone love you but I did try to put things right, only to find myself in a world of uncertainty. There was no going back.

Stage 4 – Depression

Depression for me was like the devil. I locked myself away from the world, the window blinds shut, and I became a prisoner in my own home.

Stage 5 – Acceptance

During bereavement we go to all stages for a certain amount of time, experiencing different levels of intensity. They will not be in any particular order and you will visit the stages until you are ready to accept and let go.

Not everyone will experience all stages as it depends on each individual; we all deal with loss differently.

Unlike a death, he was alive, living another life with someone else, living close by, and carrying on with his life with my 'replacement'.

I kept my distance from any interaction but occasionally my texts turned into rages and eventually I had to cut all contact from him, for my own sanity. Avoidance worked for me, I had to take myself away from the reality of life until I could fully accept it. The pain and anger resided within me for a long time, the reason for this was that I felt I didn't get closure, I didn't get the truth and his betrayal was hard for me to come to terms with.

I admit to saying some pretty terrible things, which in my defence was the way I had to let my pain out. I honestly could not believe that he could do that and move on so quickly; we are not even divorced yet.

As part of my recovery plan, I tried to look into the future and believe that life would get better in time. A bucket list was written and on it was to bring a new addition into the family...

I had always wanted a puppy and the kids did too. So after months of isolating myself from the world, I soon as I knew that my foot was recovering and I would be able to get about (finally) we brought Layla home.

She was a tiny Shih Tzu pedigree with black hair, nose and eyes..... Utterly adorable and the perfect addition to our family.

It's been a few weeks since she became part of our lives and she has taken over the household with her personality and playful ways. We can't remember life without her. We are still in the potty training stage, which is a challenge, but I wouldn't change it for the world.

I have read that dogs help to ease anxiety and stress, they become a big part of the family and she has definitely been a positive influence on our lives so far.

She is my morning alarm and every day she wakes between 5 - 5:30am. The morning routine we have together is that I sit with her in the garden while she runs around and sniffs and chews everything in sight before her first piddle of the day.

I have set up my laptop in the kitchen where I can get back to documenting my day to day life. I spend the next few hours writing and a never forget my workout; burst training on a stationary bike which I purchased to try to help me to get my fitness back in my safe place, while my foot recovered. The thought of joining a gym freaked me out. I put my own program to the test and the results are awesome.

Layla sits beside me, she is my little ray of sunshine and brightens my day - this is my new life and it's going in the right direction.

At 9 weeks old, Layla started to fetch her ball but still continued to soil the house. I found myself constantly picking up dog turds before she ate them... urgh this was all new to me and like a newborn baby she had to learn along the way. Plans to finish my book by the deadline were doubtful, puppy potty training was a little harder than expected but hopefully won't take long for her to grasp.

I started to appreciate the smallest of things, as I sat in the garden watching her play and investigate her surroundings, I noticed that I could smell the air, I could hear the birds, I could feel myself filling up with gratitude and the realisation that my life was great and can only get better. These things are what we take for granted and I hadn't noticed any of them in a long time. It was as if all of my senses were numb but they all came back to me and I started to appreciate them even more. Sounds strange but it made me feel alive.

I also made a decision to stop taking my anti-depressants; it's all or nothing with me.

I knew this was a risk but I was determined to do this on my own. I had lots of therapy sessions in the past which put another perspective on my situation, however, re-living the past didn't work for me. Everyone is different and I would never tell anyone to make the same decision without talking to your GP or therapist first.

I had tried to come off the meds a few times before and found myself climbing the walls and falling deeper into depression. It was like one step forward and two steps back. You think you have turned a corner then bam you feel worse than you ever did. It was brutal. I remember thinking that I would never recover, I really believed that and it terrified me.

They were counterproductive, I was so unhappy with my weight gain, I felt a mess and being so overweight was not helping me to get out of the house, therefore becoming even more isolated. I was stuck in a rut with the option of staying on the meds and turn into a sumo or come off the meds and go bonkers crazy. I work out daily and it's still such a struggle to feel good about myself when none of my clothes fit me. I squeeze into my size 12 joggers that make me resemble a witchetty grub. I am not the person I want to be in this body.

It has taken me a long time to beat my demons down and now that I was excited for the future and taking action to live a better life, the meds had to go.

The first few weeks I noticed that my negative thoughts were starting to dominate my mind yet again; I suffered headaches, increased anxiety, insomnia and fatigue all the bad shit that I wanted to run from. I am determined to see it through this time but I am still feeling the symptoms of withdrawal as my body and mind adjust.

I have changed my day-to-day life completely by sticking with positive activities and filling my head with happy thoughts, I am still battling everyday but I am implementing action, small daily tasks that result in positive change.

Into my 3rd week off the meds and waves of emotion still come over me, I cry most days but not all are sad tears. I am noticing that sticking to my new schedule is really paying off. I feel stronger, I am more in control of my feelings and I am focused on reaching my goals and never looking back.

I have studied the Law of Attraction for many months now and pursued a consistent path of finding my way to happiness and abundance.

The only problem was that I never really could free myself from the way I felt about what had happened to me. I was making my life miserable.

Let me tell you that it is so easy to be on the outside looking in at people who are on the road of self-destruction. The woe is me and self-pity cycle of hopelessness. Couldn't you just shake those people and tell them to get a fucking grip! Let it go and move on with your life for god sake you are only hurting yourself and those around you that care.

Well that's all well and good for the people witnessing the devastating effects of someone losing it all - I spent most of my life having an optimistic outlook and never thought that I would have to endure such pain and distress that my separation/divorce inflicted upon me. I blamed everyone and everything on external circumstance when all along; all that I had to do was get myself out of the darkness and into the light. I inflicted unbearable pain upon myself but until I actually 'got it' then I would continue this path until I was old and grey, if I ever lived that long!

Chapter Seven: Spanish Adventure... HOLA!

The following days I felt on fire with happy vibes and positive plans to move forward and what came to me next was quite unexpected, I still felt like Groundhog Day in the house, even though I did feel a lot happier, I still felt stuck and a bit uninspired to get pen to paper again. If only I could stop this constant cycle of falling back into chaos?

Lots of people knew about the book and I had orders lining up months ago which I seemed to have forgotten all about until recently. Don't get me wrong, I don't think I am the next JK Rowling (even though I have joked about it) but something comes alive in me when I write, it does something to me like nothing else.

Writing a book about yourself is actually quite terrifying and to expose my vulnerability has at times been a little too hard to bear. I felt myself slipping into the cycle of self-doubt and dissecting every chapter, sentence and word. Aw fuck it! What can be worse? Erm.... not accomplishing my book at all and leaving it unpublished, unfinished and undiscovered? DERRR so after reminding myself that I'm a freaking rock star, I decided (yet again) that this time I will finish the bloody book!

Anyway back to the actual title of this chapter... SPAIN! Have you noticed that I tend to go off on one? Ok blame my undiagnosed mood disorder that I self-diagnosed myself following months of studying my extreme highs and lows, my personality cartwheels and diving into the shallow end of the pool moments that obviously became magnified by being lied to and cheated on but hey I aren't the professional and self-diagnosis is not recommended kids!

The last chapter of my book had to be finished on a high, after all, it was in the title 'The Comeback' says it all really, surely you have to comeback with bells on don't you? Which is obviously my intention – Dingaling Dong!

So, you guessed it, I randomly booked a flight to get some headspace in order to finish 'the said book' thinking that the sun, sea and sangria would inspire me in the same way that my trip to Ibiza did.

When dad met me at the airport I bet he was thinking... god what have I got to deal with here? I rang him the day before to ask if I could stay for a while to get my shit together and accomplish this one thing that was holding me back. It wasn't even about the book sales that were driving me; it was the love of writing and expressing my thoughts in ways that lifted me up.

It feels surreal, just landing in Spain the very next day that I had the idea to jet off for a bit. I hoped it wasn't 'one of my episodes' and that I was not going to lose the plot while I was here. Crikey, this spontaneous urge to leave for some 'me time' better work. It feels like my last shot.

I greeted my dad with a hug and an Adios' yep I think I am well funny at times. Daddy-daughter time I said to him with a smile on my face from ear to ear. Shit I have actually travelled to another country to find myself, fair play I was coming into a safe place, somewhere familiar to me and of course daddykins was here and we were going to spend some overly due one on one time, now if anything good comes from this trip I know that hanging out with the big fella was going to inject some deep gratitude into my system and boost my mood whatever the outcome.

So with no distractions, no stress, no food binges and alcohol, just me focused on my wellbeing, I decided what better time to test run my new 4 day retreat program which was designed for women just like me, women who had lost their way in life by a traumatic life changing experience and were left feeling worthless, hopeless and a million other crappy emotions.

I started to feel different in myself, chilled, happy and very optimistic that finally, my dreams will become a reality. I am looking forward to the future life I had planned for so long but they were only dreams up until now because now I have taken the action needed to make it happen and forget the past forever.

Staying with dad will hopefully be the one thing that helps me get my life back (and then some).

He mentioned that he feeds a dog every morning at 9am, he lives in a block of apartments and sure enough on the dot, I heard barking, it was Benji asking for his treat. As I looked over the balcony to wish him good morning, I thought of Layla straight away, we only had her short time but I miss her so much. Although I had a relapse and was too ill to give her the care and attention she deserved, it was with such a heavy heart that we had to re home her.

She did have a positive effect on my state of mind and I remember the moment I started to notice and appreciate the simple things again.

I am over the moon with her new owners, she settled in immediately and I was sent photographs and video clips of her playing with her new big sister Rosie. I did feel like it was something else I failed at but that was the old me, the one who beat myself up for everything bad in my life, blaming myself and feeling that whatever I put my mind to, it never turned out how I'd hoped.

I wanted to make it clear to dad that I came here to work and it was not a holiday for me, however tempting it was to go back to my old ways. The first night, I insisted he do whatever he had planned and that I don't want to be any disruption. I called him without warning literally hours ago so I was going to ensure that I worked my fingers to the bone before heading back home again.

I scheduled time to write, to learn, to exercise and to eat well. A meticulous plan to keep me focused on my end goal.

To make the most of my trip, I thought that I would arrange a few viewings of some millionaire cribs to rent for my new business venture. I surfed the net to find some corkers.

Returning home knowing that I had accomplished what I set out to achieve began to sink in and I became super motivated. It was another missing part of the puzzle and to reconnect to what matters and make life the best it's ever been!

Spain is where my personal growth journey starts where I can focus on me myself and I, failing so many times before in 'the real world' I took a last shot to get myself to where I want to be. The only thing to do was to cut myself away from any distractions.

I focused on changing my thinking and eating habits intensively to overcome the cycle that I became victim to far too many times. Inspiration comes from many things but I took myself on a spiritual journey

My third day into the plan and I feel ever so slightly deflated, I don't think I will be going back home with a six pack put it that way. My swollen kite has reduced by about a tenth of a millimetre but at least slow progress is better than no progress!

Gulping down gallons of water is working magic on my skin and I'm off the vino to get down to business. I have not sun bathed in the golden sunshine sipping on tequilas, however tempting it was.

Chapter Eight – Too hard on myself

That's my trouble. I put so much pressure on myself to achieve a million things at the same time so it all ends up back to where I started feeling like a failure. So how am I going to stop my bad habits and finally succeed in something?

I planned to spread the book out into parts so I could take the pressure off and concentrate on getting the first part out there, I had too much going on in my head and decided to work on my personal transformation comeback once I had completed my first book.

I will be documenting my progress which will offer the tips and tricks I implemented to regain my confidence, lose weight and get fit in the comfort of my own home.

It will be designed to help other women who suffer with obesity, low self- esteem, social anxiety and depression. A transformative program to get your Bootylicious back!

Anxiety and depression stripped me down and I became an empty shell, isolating myself and fearing that if I stepped outside, something awful would happen. I spent hours reading and learning every day. Some days I couldn't take in a single word as my thoughts raced uncontrollably.

Trapped and unable to work, I decided to start looking after myself, I needed a rocket up my arse to get started but I had to do something. I felt miserable.

Implementing small and achievable daily tasks was the only way forward.

During the next few months I suffered a few setbacks and became unwell again. Thankfully the episodes were shorter and not as intense. I was beginning to control my emotions a lot better than I used to.

A little at a time I was moving closer to feeling better and wanted to get back in the game, I had worked so hard over the past five years and despite my failures I never lost passion and faith in that one day my hard work will pay off but all it done for me was drive my husband away with some persistent persuasion from who he ended up with.

Trying to make him happy and build a better life for us was so hard but I kept pushing through, believing that one day, my business would flourish and we would all live happily ever after.

I spent half of my life with my significant other and the thought of facing life without him was something I never thought I would have to face. I did fall to pieces, my life turned into a living hell but I fought through it nonetheless.

Chapter Nine: Accepting and moving on

It was a long road to acceptance. I thought I reached it many times before, only to fall back into the same re-numerating thoughts of being a victim of my circumstances.

Every day is a new day and I appreciate that I have come so far and that I can finally feel excited about my future and know in my heart that I can create my own world.

When someone you love becomes a stranger and chooses someone else over you, it leaves you broken. Some people don't get over such heartache and live an empty life, not me; I have wasted enough time over thinking and feeling sorry for myself.

I had to find myself before I could make any necessary changes to my life. I had to accept that I was now single, my marriage was now in the past and I realised that trying to change my body shape, lifestyle and mindset was going to happen in gradual stages.

A whole year later and the final chapter of part one of my adventures is about to be unravelled.

How heartbreak can turn you into someone else, they say that writers do their best work in the struggle along with singers and artists ... I am no Adele so I will stick to writing but I do a good impersonation of Phoebe from friends' smelling cat... What a ledge! Anyway, talking is my favourite past time (who da guessed)??

I done something amazing today, I felt very proud of myself actually!

My old fitness studio 'Bootylicious Bootcamps' turned into a tattoo place when my lease was over. I had wanted an iddy biddy ink on my finger for a while, however tempting it was to get it on the middle finger, I chose the finger which had a dent from the wedding rings I wore for 17 years, they were long gone.

I was unable to bring myself to go into Bootylicious again for the fear of crying a river or having a meltdown, but when I returned home from Spain, I felt it was symbolic to get the tattoo done where the beginning of the end all started and to draw a line under the past forever. It was closure on my failed marriage and my failed business. Instead of feeling sad, I felt empowered.

So there I was having some banter with the lads in there, I said to them 'you wouldn't believe the amount of burpees I have done on this floor' it broke the ice and I told them the reasons behind my tattoo, I talked my face off because that's what I do best and they got my life story within 5 minutes. I came out feeling freakin fabulous and turned into one of those excited fiancé's who had just been proposed to holding out my hand proud as punch with admiration.

I had definitely turned a corner (another one) Jeez this path called life sure has had some wrong turns but this time I was on the right path. The path always meant for me and I skipped into the sunset with a big chuffing smile on my face.

The tattoo is a semicolon, which represents mental illness; something that I have experienced on so many levels over the years but it was my recent descent that totally destroyed me from within. A very poignant symbol meaning 'My story isn't over' I could of ended my life during my darkest days but I chose not to and only those who have been to that same place can truly understand the despair and the belief that there really is no way out. So please be kind, do not assume that the road to recovery is easy. Sadly some don't make their way back to get another chance at life but the collective support of my family, friends and professionals helped me to get my life back. Time is a great healer and you have to give yourself plenty of time to appreciate what is on the other side of pain.

So here it is, on my hand for all to see, breaking the stigma and giving some hope to other sufferers. Wearing it proudly, as a sign of my own courage. My rise from the ashes as I picked up the pieces of my broken self to continue to fight another day a stronger better version of me... I've only gone and done it!

Chapter Ten: Time to reflect

In life, we all experience heartache, obstacles will always be out there to test us, to strengthen us and the choices we make are part of our own personal journey. We create our own world. We can make it wonderful by living in the present moment and appreciate it for all that it is. We do overcome bad times and nothing in life stays the same. I feared change but I pushed through every day and I now stand-alone much stronger.

I want people to know that even at your lowest times, there is light past the darkness and you will come out a much better person from it.

Take your time to find yourself, find something to be thankful for in everyday and learn how to control your own emotions; these emotions are brought on by your own thoughts. You are the one putting yourself through bad times so choose to be happy, choose to become all that you want to be. It is your life and your responsibility to live it well.

So how did I come from despair to repair?

I got through it somehow, I am never looking back and painful memories will always resurface but they begin to fade. It takes some graft but never give up. Do more of what you love every day fill your days with laughter, adventure and day dreams.

I look back at how far I have come, how I have turned my life around and followed my dreams even through the toughest moments I got back up.

If my story inspired you, I do hope it has, take something from it and apply it to your life. Believe in yourself even if no one else   does.
Learn to love yourself- Live again - When someone you love with all of your heart rejects you, you feel like no one will ever love you again, you feel broken and for me, I couldn't look in the mirror. I was repulsed at what was staring back at me. I had savaged my body with stress and worry and my eating habits had turned me into another person. Out of control, I hated myself.

Months of self-sabotage and torment had compounded my negative feelings. I failed to get fit and start looking after myself. I would manage a week to 10 days then fall back into the cycle of doom and gloom!

I didn't care anymore; I was hibernating.

Then something clicked and I thought to myself, Get back up and get your life back, only you can do it.

After lots of self-help videos and heaps of research, I started to take control of my life and start caring for me. I needed to take care of myself; I felt unhealthy, stressed and hated how I was living, I was stuck in a bad place for a long time.

I know that I still have a long way to go, although we split so long ago, the realisation of never getting back together again didn't truly hit me until him moving on with someone else came to light. In his eyes, our marriage was over long before we separated and he was probably relieved when I left.

It's been 9 months now since the day I found out straight from the horses mouth via social media and I have read about some people never recovering from divorce, some take years but I hope that the pain no longer creeps into my everyday life. It is getting easier to live with; some days are better than others.

Finally letting go of my husband has enabled me to carry on, building my new life and losing myself for over a year has made me appreciate the amazing people around me but unfortunately, they can't prevent another relapse.

It's so easy to look at your future in a positive way when you are happy with your life as it is. The struggle is finding positivity from under the dark clouds. That is where the courage lies. Pulling yourself up from the floor repeatedly.

I do consider myself a badass and I will continue to fight each day and find my purpose, following dreams alone instead of with who I wished to share my future with. It's a bitter pill to swallow being rejected and betrayed - ignored like I never existed. Was it any wonder that I lost my mind and fell into major depression? Being replaced by someone on your own doorstep has to be up there as one of the shittiest experiences I have encountered. So here is the thing. I had every right to be enraged by my circumstances and the deceit I was so cruelly subjected to but feeling resentment for so long was only hurting me.

As a mother, you want the best for your children. During my tough times, my depression was so bad that my mum had them stay with her. I didn't want them to be around me while I was not myself. The person I was some days frightened me never mind how they must feel seeing me so unwell? What all this does to them? I worry about their future.

My boys behaviour is increasingly changing, however, he knows that his mum is poorly. I isolate myself from everyone and then feel guilty for not seeing my children.

I am so grateful for the family and friends who checked up on me while I was so poorly. Not many were aware of how serious my mental illness actually was. I wasn't just suffering from a broken heart, I couldn't just 'get over him' and I wasn't interested in going out with other people.

I was living in a world of fear and pain and when people said things like 'you know where I am' and 'pop over or a cuppa anytime' these words were irrelevant. I couldn't even function and get out of bed some days; I couldn't leave my own home some days because every day I was left terrified of the outside world.

They weren't to know how debilitating my life had become and I didn't want to burden them with my problems. I wasn't attention seeking, I kept myself very isolated because the person I had become was unrecognisable.

It's exactly a year this month that I received the Facebook message from a 'Fake friend' taking great pleasure in destroying my world with her words.

To say I took the betrayal badly is an understatement but rather than fess up, they made up a story to convince me that they had only just started to see each other as more than friends.

It has taken time but I have taken control of my life on my terms and couldn't give a shit anymore, in fact looking back she done me a real favour and she obviously needs my husband more than I do so I wish them both well I really do (something I would never have said only months ago).

It has taken me a whole year to step up and get ready for my new transformation, this time on a whole new level. Nothing will bring me down as I plan my future and take the action needed to see it through and welcome all the setbacks because I know they only make me stronger.

The shift in my mindset is like a bolt of lightning, a sudden realisation that my life is in my own hands and I can have whatever I want, I just needed the courage to go for it.

Miracles do happen so it seems.

Find out what Jayne did next... The Comeback; Part 2: OPEN LETTER TO MY EX – out in 2018!

It was always the little things that pulled at my heart strings when we first spilt - I would go shopping and go to pick your favourite food, songs on the radio, I would even look at clothes that would suit you and suddenly the reality hit me that you were no longer in my life.

I am reminded every anniversary, birthday and special occasion. When I take the kids out, I can only see happy families together, it is so upsetting and I still think of you every day.

I missed cooking for you; I know I was far from a domestic goddess but I tried my best to make you happy.

Your life hardly changed compared to mine, I had to start my life over, moving from the family home we shared for 17 years.
You gained a new relationship and your life pretty much stayed the same until the house was sold.

The sacrifices I had to make because you wouldn't leave and you made me feel guilty for working too hard and neglecting you.
Not only did I work endlessly to provide us with a better life, I also worked for you, I was a mother, a wife and loved you unconditionally only for you to move on with someone else on your own doorstep.

Of course I was reeling from your betrayal and yes I lashed out at you! You destroyed me and walked away from our marriage.

You blamed me and you thought that I had been putting myself about. The last thing I wanted was to throw myself at strangers for kicks. You think that keeping the truth from me will hurt me less when all it has done is caused more pain. Tormented thoughts that led me to hit rock bottom and stay there for a long time.

If you were honest with me then I could have accepted the truth and got over it eventually without being left to think all sorts about when you two started your deceitful relationship.

Having you in my life is still so painful so I keep my distance. I will never forget the loss I felt. People say 'but you have two kids' 'you need to get on for their sake' maybe in time.

You have taken away so much from me. I cannot allow you to hurt me again so I choose to stay away. You collect the kids every day to take them to school because my anxiety triggers from the bad memories that still hold me down. I don't look out of the window, if I do see your car it makes me angry. I wish I could be free from you but it seems impossible.

It took a while to see things from another perspective and move on from the hurt. I no longer blame myself; it was your choice to go off with someone else but I was to blame, which was your excuse to cover up the truth, to make what you did acceptable.

104

I am trying so hard to forgive you and slowly the fire is burning out. What is left of our marriage is a pile of dust. I have been through the grieving cycle of losing you as if you were dead. It probably hurts more because you are still living your life without me, with someone else but I never stopped loving you despite everything.

Now I have been through this experience I know that I don't need you in my life. I am saddened that all those years together were pushed aside as if they never existed.

You made your own choices and I was left to pick up the pieces feeling humiliated that I loved you so much but it was all one sided.

Not taking responsibility for your actions did leave me feeling disappointed and let down by the one person I thought I would spend the rest of my life with.

Thankfully I don't lay awake at night anymore missing you or feeling lonely, I don't need a man in my life. I had a brief fling with an old friend but I'm not ready for another relationship, I want to live my life full of adventure, to travel the world and to take the kids to magical places.

They are my priority as were you but you think the grass is greener, I hope for your sake it is and now instead of feeling empty I am feeling grateful for the years we spent together and the beautiful children we brought into the world.

I wish you well and hope that you live a happy life x

Acknowledgements

With thanks to:

Steve Wharton who introduced me to High Vibrational Thinking and inspired me to write;

Sunray Media for my book design and tech support;

Dave Brooks for editing and helping publish this book;

Teesside Crisis Team, Alliance and my GP for providing mental health care and advice;

Family and friends for supporting me throughout in particular those who lived through every day with me; and

My mum, dad, best friend Anna, and my children as they were my reason to carry on.

22499810R00069

Printed in Great Britain
by Amazon